HAL•LEONARD
INSTRUMENTAL
PLAY-ALONG

AUDIO
ACCESS
INCLUDED

PLAYBACK+
:d • Pitch • Balance • Loop

TRUMPET IN B♭

WEST SIDE STORY

T0082975

Based on a conception of Jerome Robbins

Book by
Arthur Laurents

Music by
Leonard Bernstein®

Lyrics by
Stephen Sondheim

Entire Original Production
Directed and Choreographed by
Jerome Robbins

ISBN 978-1-4234-5827-2

To access companion recorded audio, visit:
www.halleonard.com/mylibrary

Enter Code
7027-9042-3843-1123

LEONARD
BERNSTEIN
Music Publishing
Company LLC

BOOSEY & HAWKES

DISTRIBUTED BY

HAL•LEONARD®

Visit Hal Leonard Online at
www.halleonard.com

Contact us:
Hal Leonard
7777 West Bluemound Road
Milwaukee, WI 53213
Email: info@halleonard.com

In Europe, contact:
Hal Leonard Europe Limited
42 Wigmore Street
Marylebone, London, W1U 2RN
Email: info@halleonardeurope.com

In Australia, contact:
Hal Leonard Australia Pty. Ltd.
4 Lentara Court
Cheltenham, Victoria, 3192 Australia
Email: info@halleonard.com.au

CONTENTS

The price of this publication includes access to companion recorded audio online, for download or streaming, using the unique code found on the title page. Visit **www.halleonard.com/mylibrary** and enter the access code.

A melody cue is included on the right channel only which may be adjusted up or down to hear the accompaniment or full version.

◆ AMERICA

TRUMPET IN B♭

Lyrics by STEPHEN SONDHEIM
Music by LEONARD BERNSTEIN

◆ COOL

TRUMPET IN B♭

Lyrics by STEPHEN SONDHEIM
Music by LEONARD BERNSTEIN

❸ I FEEL PRETTY

TRUMPET IN B♭

Lyrics by STEPHEN SONDHEIM
Music by LEONARD BERNSTEIN

I HAVE A LOVE

TRUMPET IN B♭

Lyrics by STEPHEN SONDHEIM
Music by LEONARD BERNSTEIN

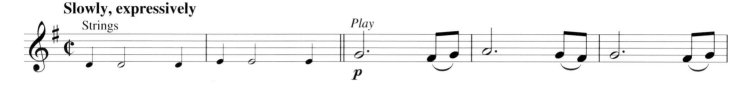

◆ ⑤ JET SONG

TRUMPET IN B♭

Lyrics by STEPHEN SONDHEIM
Music by LEONARD BERNSTEIN

◆ MARIA

TRUMPET IN B♭

Lyrics by STEPHEN SONDHEIM
Music by LEONARD BERNSTEIN

❼ ONE HAND, ONE HEART

TRUMPET IN B♭

Lyrics by STEPHEN SONDHEIM
Music by LEONARD BERNSTEIN

◆⑧ SOMETHING'S COMING

TRUMPET IN B♭

Lyrics by STEPHEN SONDHEIM
Music by LEONARD BERNSTEIN

◆ 9 SOMEWHERE

TRUMPET IN B♭

Lyrics by STEPHEN SONDHEIM
Music by LEONARD BERNSTEIN

◆10 TONIGHT

TRUMPET IN B♭

Lyrics by STEPHEN SONDHEIM
Music by LEONARD BERNSTEIN